Praise for *Hawk on Wire*

"Scott Starbuck's *Hawk on Wire: Ecopoems* doesn't flinch or compromise. From his considerable experience with of the wild world comes a grim projection of our future, thanks mainly to our own ravishing of it. But this grim vision is usually accompanied by the beckoning of a spirit world beyond impending disaster. So it is in these mainly aphoristic poems, some of which feature ghosts of already passed-away luminaries speaking of climate change, such as Galileo and Mother Teresa. The ghost of Charles Bukowski admonishes us by saying 'we must find / some way // to make joy / no matter what.' This is a wonderful, bracing, and searching book, lovingly and expertly written."
—John Keeble, author of *Yellowfish*, *Broken Ground*, and *The Shadows of Owls*

"Traditionally conceived, a poet is not only a maker but a prophet, a vates or shaman. Prophecies are traditionally riddling and ambiguous, subject to tragic misinterpretation. But the prescient lyrics of *Hawk on Wire* have an urgent clarity, which reminds us that ecopoetry, whatever else it is, must include ecoprophecy. Shifting from the lyric present into the cataclysmic future, or dreaming back from post-apocalyptic end-times, Starbuck divines the consequences of climate change in no uncertain terms. Yet more than foretelling, this fisherman poet listens: to the ghosts of elders and outcasts (Mother Teresa, Mark Twain, Galileo, the homeless), to fellow creatures (trout, lizard, otter, hawk) and to the elements (earth, river, wind). Ecologists read the signs of unsustainability, poets give them voice, none more compellingly than Starbuck. The question remains, can we look up from our screens long enough to listen?"
—John Shoptaw, author of *Times Beach*

"Orwell, Twain, Rilke, Mother Theresa, Galileo, and Martha, the last passenger pigeon, are among the ghosts who speak of climate change in Scott T. Starbuck's solastalgic *Hawk on Wire*. Their voices haunt Starbuck's landscapes and riverscapes, where he casts for steelhead. In the face of greed, willful ignorance, and 'alternative facts,' Starbuck's activist poetry is needed more than ever."
—Eric Magrane, coeditor of *The Sonoran Desert: A Literary Field Guide*

"For the reality of nature, we must go to poets like Starbuck who base their passions on what the scientists tell them. Aptly, Starbuck writes in his poem, 'Election Year': 'A trout pauses / over a nickel // maybe thinking / it's food // then darts / into darkness / / maybe recording / face and date // in its unconscious / mind, // its blinking dreams, / the way humans / / hear of melting / Arctic, // blink, and do/ nothing.' Reading *Hawk on Wire* is a way of sharing love, concern, and joy in the natural world and her dwindling wildlife. I recommend this book as a way of finding solace in sharing warning, wonder and joy."
—Daniela Gioseffi, American Book Award winning author, Editor: www.Eco-Poetry.org

"*Hawk on Wire* by Scott T. Starbuck is an essential collection of poetry. The poems in this collection ask the reader to dig deeper into her/his existence in connection with the natural world and each other. They remind us about the preciousness of what we are losing as we are 'putting all life in a train to a cliff.' Each of Starbuck's poems in this collection is a gem, lyrical and full of clarity, as if one is looking at a diamond in the palm of one's hand and its truth is unbreakable. Starbuck writes, 'Some never returned to nature / until cremated ashes // floated downriver / or were lifted by wind.' Perhaps, it is time now for each one of us to return to Mother Earth before our deaths. Starbuck writes about climate change and mass extinction. In his title poem, 'Hawk on Wire,' Starbuck writes, 'Hawk on wire / avoids me / flying ahead / from pole to pole // until there are / no more poles / like wild things // fleeing acidic seas / melting glaciers /drought, // track makers' / wicked machines.' Starbuck has a profound bond with the natural world. His poems awaken us from a deep sleep."
—Teresa Mei Chuc, author of the poetry collections *Red Thread* and *Keeper of the Winds*

"Scott Starbuck's ecopoems are light-filled gems of the human spirit, wrought half from tears of delight, half from sorrow. A true world citizen, Starbuck speaks across time and space in these haunting meditations on the beauties and fragility of our planet. Tuned to his deep-listening ear, we can eavesdrop on our wisest ancestral voices, from T'ao Ch'ien to Galileo, Chief Charlie DePoe to Charles Bukowski. To read this collection is to enter the heart of the world, with its back door wide open to the mystery."
—Prartho Sereno, prize-winning author of *Elephant Raga* and *Call From Paris*

"Scott T. Starbuck's poems are genuine lyrics, artfully delivered, that speak to us about the value of human life and environment. He does not shy away from the tough and urgent ecological questions. With keen observations his poems carry messages from numerous and eclectic sources, including hieroglyphics, Oregon landscapes, fish, the spirit of wind, and a parking lot prophet. With wit and intelligence, Starbuck also includes a variety of ghosts (from Socrates to Bukowski) commenting on climate change. His poems are informative, imaginative, and wise."
—Michael Spring, author of *Unfolding the Field*

"Scott's poems are crisp, visual, sharp, no wasted words, every word carrying its fair share of a meaning beyond itself. His love for all the living things made of the planet's ingredients is palpable, understated, and poignant. Take 'Punch Bowl Hike Meditation': 'For 30 years / I've talked to myself / about climate change / but now most everyone is. // When you think that long / you feel for / Nina in flower garden, / sparrow on fence.'" Gail Entrekin, Editor, *Canary* (canarylitmag.org)

"Interspersed with salmon fishing and Starbuck's ghosts – Mother Teresa, Galileo, Twain and many others – *Hawk on Wire* deftly challenges and invites its readers to respond to anthropogenic climate change. In Starbuck's world, nine-year-old's 'were still whole enough / to sit on a hill and cry' as 'developers destroyed our valley.' Images of pathos, 'a roadkill map // to nowhere,' are poised against irony, and a sense that other paths were and are possible, 'if we had not / taken that joyride / with the guys / in the stolen car.' Despite the bleakness of the present, Bukowski's ghost asserts: 'we must find / some way // to make joy / no matter what.' In these engaging ecopoems, otherkind call to humankind in an 'ancient voice, / old as missing rain,' that 'says look, look, look.'"
—Anne Elvey, Managing Editor, *Plumwood Mountain: An Australian Journal of Ecopoetry and Ecopoetics*

"These terse, urgent poems, part parable, part prophecy, implore us to 'look, look, look' at changes we're causing to ecosystems and landscapes around us. Read them now to feel the cold splash of water on our faces that we need to wake up."
—Daniel Hudon, author of *Brief Eulogies for Lost Animals*

"Scott T. Starbuck's *Hawk on Wire* offers the hard truth on climate change and forces the question of whether art has the responsibility for advocating political positions. It does, and these poems do advocate — pointedly, crisply, and with no doubt as to our role and responsibility in catastrophic environmental change. Starbuck's is a necessary truth, one we must rally behind if we are 'to fight with your time and words / for your children,' as he writes. In this brutally honest collection, the craft is as sharp as the words. And that's precisely what we need today, because it won't be a 'plaid and denim prophet' who saves us, nor any prophet at all. It will only be us, a fiercely sharp willingness to defend the planet, '[e]ach country committed to saving / one thing from extinction — them.'"
—Simmons B. Buntin, author of *Bloom, Riverfall,* and *Unsprawl* and editor-in-chief of Terrain.org

"In what is truly a place-based book (Chewaucan River, Oregon) that focuses on the larger story of climate change, and with the voice of a storyteller whose message and imagery transcends the obvious with some poems reading like parables, Scott Starbuck urges us to 'venture beyond Facebook' and 'to be there / you have to turn off the TV / and go outside.' And herein lies the true essence of this book—that 'we are not here to take more than we need' but to think and live sustainably, **with** nature, with care, and with kindness. After all is said and done in this must-read Eco-classic with an important message for our time, Starbuck leaves us with a simple mantra and an ancient koan imploring us to 'Look, look, look' and 'to make joy / no matter what.'"
—Thomas Rain Crowe, author of *Zoro's Field: My Life in the Appalachian Woods*

"Starbuck's *Hawk on Wire* is a poetic gift alerting us to what is happening to our planet; we must listen and act before it is too late."
—Yun Wang, Senior Research Scientist at IPAC Caltech, and author of *The Book of Totality* and Nicholas Roerich Poetry Prize Winner *The Book of Jade*

Hawk on Wire

Ecopoems

Scott T. Starbuck

Fomite
Burlington, VT

Copyright © 2017 Scott T. Starbuck

All rights reserved. No part of this book may be reproduced in any form or by any means without the prior written consent of the publisher, except in the case of brief quotations used in reviews and certain other noncommercial uses permitted by copyright law.

Cover Art © Guy Denning
Jophiel Watches - conte and chalk on paper, 80 x 40 cm

ISBN-978-1-944388-05-8
Library of Congress Control Number: 2017935696

"We are part fire, and part dream." — Fire Dog, Cheyenne

Contents

In Paisley 1
Election Year 2
Punch Bowl Hike Meditation 3
Wind Spirit 4
Conundrum 5
Nov. 28, 2015 – One Man Climate March
    at PLAYA, Oregon 6
Thoughts at the End of Empire 7
Climate Prophet 8
Remembering Chief Charlie DePoe Who Loved Trains 9
Ghost of Mother Teresa Speaks
    of Need for Planetary Grief 10
Ghost of Galileo Speaks of Climate Change 11
Initiation Poem 12
Ghost of Ed Abbey Speaks of Climate Change 13
Hawk on Wire 14
Ghost of T'ao Ch'ien Speaks of Climate Change 15
Geo-Poem 16
Why, Unless Things Change Soon, We May Lose on Climate 17
Staring at PLAYA Pond Thinking of Impermanence 18
Ghost of Bukowski Speaks of Climate Change 19
How We Stopped Corporate Psychopaths
    From Cooking Planet Earth 20
2007 Logos 21
After Dreaming Extinction of Birds 22
Desert Time Machine 23
The Self at North Fork Lake Splits into Three Selves 24
The Day I Stopped the Rape at Church Camp 25
Shad Fishers 26
Ludicrous 27
History Lesson 28

Climate Poem	29
Disabled Dancer	30
Reframe, Redefine	31
Water Cave Near Mogollon Rim	32
Indian Boy	33
Things I Learned at Blue River Writers Gathering	34
Near Paisley, Oregon	36
Ghost of Mark Twain Speaks of Climate Change	37
Great Horned Owl	38
Ghost of Orwell Speaks of Climate Change	39
Seven Things I Saw Near Borrego Desert	40
The River That Flows Through Town	41
Message from Far Away	42
Enkidu Moment	43
Ghost of Rilke Speaks of Climate Change	44
Why I Wait	45
Ghost of Socrates Speaks of Climate Change	46
Bud Pernell's House	47
Broken Ritual	48
Reckoning	49
By the Light of Dead Stars on the Oregon Coast	50
Warrior Says She Comes from the Land of Scalded Souls	51
What Happened	52
Poem for Kwas Enna	53
Global Warming (Gary Weber) Dream	54
Scant Light	55
Intruder	56
Lizard	57
When Fishing Was Slow	58
Chilkoot	59
The Old Ones at Coastal Creek	60
Turtle Island People	61
Exoskeleton	62
The Last Wild Otter Near Otter Crest, Oregon, 1906	63

Sparkle	64
Columbia River Pipe Nightmare	65
One Frog	66
Walking the Mountain Trail	67
Desert Wind	68
Wind Chimes at Lazy Hummingbird Café 3/17/17	69
Moonfish	70
Thinking About Our Space Program	71
Salmon Fly Fireworks	72
Night Thoughts on Brain Science	73
Things I Learned at Camp Canyonview in 6th Grade Outdoor School	74
The Radical Surgery of Now	75
Canyon	76
Acknowledgments	79
About the Author	83

In Paisley

In the library a woman grieves a troubled child.
Others speak of cows, horses, family.

The talk in Homestead Café is fishing
which I understand.

The Saloon listens quietly to a cowboy
jilted lover

while rodeo stars and angelic women
adorn ceiling and walls.

A sign over the highway notes the last
full week of July is Mosquito Festival

and I think of upriver ghosts
and the Big Mosquito Festival no one talks about.

Election Year

A trout pauses
over a nickel

maybe thinking
it's food

then darts
into darkness

maybe recording
face and date

in its unconscious
mind,

its blinking dreams,
the way humans

hear of melting
Arctic,

blink, and do
nothing.

Punch Bowl Hike Meditation

For 30 years
I've talked to myself
about climate change
but now most everyone is.

When you think that long
you feel for
Nina in flower garden,
sparrow on fence.

Wind Spirit

Wind Spirit said to the man, "I will ask a question,
and each day you give the wrong answer, I take a finger.
The question is hard, requiring much reflection,
and self-purification. I don't know how many fingers you will lose.
That is up to you.
"How will you save the community of species on Earth?"

"The question is too hard," protested the man.

"It has been ordained," said Wind Spirit, "and cannot be changed.
I will return tomorrow at noon."

The man knew coyote was smart so he went to ask,
but all coyotes were dead.

He knew king salmon had a bright red soul so he went to ask,
but all king salmon were dead.

He knew steelhead trout could leap waterfalls so he went to ask,
but all steelhead trout were dead.

He knew eagle had unerring vision so he went to ask,
but all eagles were dead.

Trembling, he knew cougar could be invisible, but all cougars were dead.

In ten days, the man lost all his fingers.

This is a parable written on what remains of ancient Pleistocene Lake
Chewaucan now called Summer Lake, Oregon.

Conundrum

Scientists tell us "Antarctic CO2 Hit 400 ppm
for the First Time in 4 million Years"*
putting all life in a train to a cliff.

Ghost of Martha, the last passenger pigeon
who died in 1914 in Cincinnati Zoo, said
"The hum of steel rails was the song

foretelling my death and yours,
my captivity and your insincerity instead of
no trains, no tracks, no cages."

* Brian Kahn at climatecentral.org on June 16, 2016

Nov. 28, 2015 – One Man Climate March at PLAYA, Oregon

Quail didn't know what I was doing
and avoided my gaze.

Rabbits stared.
A hawk ignored.

Cougar and coyote probably eyed me
as usual.

All beings in my community
counted on me
though none knew

as I marched in solidarity
with 785,000*
across Earth.

This Playa is what remains
of an ancient lake
and Indian tribes
where I dreamed a warning
in Martian hieroglyphs:

*Our red planet was
a bright water-blue planet.
Nothing more to say.*

*350.org estimated

Thoughts at the End of Empire

It's possible future generations will destroy
our art, literature, music, film,
and corporations, in bitterness
for allowing ecosystem collapse,

and mistrust for how many leaders
were distracted, apathetic, selfish,
ignorant, or insane with power and money.

It's possible future generations will redefine
family, community, work, value, happiness,
life, dirt, success.

It's possible education will change
from locking children in boxes
to getting them outside in tide pools,
rivers, creeks, deserts, mountains

and their community of remaining
mammals, birds, fish, amphibians,
invertebrates, reptiles, plants, trees.

It's also possible, based on our collective
behavior, there won't be future generations.

Climate Prophet

1989 in Fred Meyer parking lot
in Newport, Oregon,
 a homeless man grabbed my sleeve,
"If you don't stop sinning
this will all be underwater."

I thought he was meth-ed or nuts,
and not a plaid and denim prophet.

Remembering Chief Charlie DePoe Who Loved Trains

"Charlie DePoe, a leading man among the Indians, was a chief of the Joshua tribe and was noted for his good sense and wise councils and hospitality among the Indians. No one ever went away hungry from the home of DePoe Charlie." *Lincoln County Leader,* July 12, 1918

Who knew train engines at Toledo
would harm the Pacific sky?

Maybe it was whiskey ingenuity
of Scots leaving ancestral ground

like a strange unnatural salmon
unable to find his way home

who pretended he didn't have one
and roamed open sea

until his belly grew so large
he devoured channel buoys,

then boats, and finally at high tide
entire coastal villages.

Ghost of Mother Teresa Speaks of Need for Planetary Grief

She says if you don't make it to feeling
"My God, My God, why have you forsaken me?"
there can be no resurrection, transcendence,
healing, no skeptics to put their fingers
through your wounds.

Ghost of Galileo Speaks of Climate Change

"I knew the truth
but had more faith
in the power of reason
than was warranted

"so when Cesare Cremonini
looked through my scope
and pretended not to see
Jupiter's moons

"I learned about the clash
between reality
and ideology, later
recanted, saved my life,

"before the Roman Inquisition.
The problem now is,
not counting animals and plants,
lives of 7.5 billion."

Initiation Poem

"Corporations spend $2 billion each year targeted specifically on the young, intending to lure them into a life of unthinking consumption. [...] Young people on average can recognize over 1000 corporate logos but only a handful of plants and animals native to their places."
—David W. Orr, quoted in *Children And Nature*

Our goal was not to save the forest
and animals we knew
but to give them more time

so we jacked up pickups
and stole the wheels,

turned a tractor upside down
in a creek,

moved survey markers
around already-built homes.

We were nine so we painted our faces
like warriors and, at the end,
when developers destroyed our valley
we were still whole enough
to sit on a hill and cry.

Ghost of Ed Abbey Speaks of Climate Change

He says "Action is the antidote for despair"
then, on a local creek,
"Now hand me a fly."

Hawk on Wire

avoids me
flying ahead
from pole to pole

until there are
no more poles
like wild things

fleeing acidic seas
melting glaciers,
drought,

track makers'
wicked machines.

**Ghost of T'ao Ch'ien Speaks
of Climate Change**

"Imagining myself
in your age,
driving my old Toyota
sickens me
but I can't afford a Prius.

"When this is over
and survivors walk
across a new land bridge
everything
they can't carry
will be left behind."

Geo-Poem

66 million years ago in the Cenozoic era
seawater filled these valleys
with bass hovering like piñatas unaware

of wagon trains, cattle ranches, asphalt roads,
signs to Fort Rock and Christmas Valley
just around the pluvial corner.

Instead, bass knew only the language
of hunger, sex, territory, blankly staring
like men today watching TV.

**Why, Unless Things Change Soon,
We May Lose on Climate**

A few years ago, a black lab pup
was nearly flattened by a U-Haul
on the street where I live. I love dogs

so I wrestled her away, and my neighbor
made a leash for me to visit
80 houses to find her owner.

Some ignored my knock even though
I could see people on the couch
watching television.

Some cracked their doors in fear
before interjecting "She's not mine."
and quickly closing.

The Pacific in the distance
and manicured tropical yards
showed privilege.

Many homeowners offered encouragement
like "She's beautiful.
You are doing the right thing."

or "Keep trying."

Staring at PLAYA Pond Thinking of Impermanence

When you hold someone or something dying,
you move through layers of grief and acceptance,
grief again, acceptance, a space-time dragonfly
on a farm pond near a rope swing
as Giant Bass of Death leaps, bites, swallows,
splashing artfully invisible as whole scene
of fading planets, lovers, parents
rings in shadow of spirit angler working the water.

Ghost of Bukowski Speaks of Climate Change

"Yes, it's bleak,
bleaker than sheep snot
on barbed wire

"but, hope or no hope,
we must find
some way

"to make joy
no matter what."

How We Stopped Corporate Psychopaths From Cooking Planet Earth

—for Mary DeMocker

We planted trees everywhere at once.
Facebook posted only the words "Go outside."

"Destroy Your Television Day" grew more popular
than Xmas and the 4th of July.

Children of execs saw themselves as global citizens
and despite every temptation and distraction

disowned wayward parents.
ExxonMobil became BlueOrbSolar.

Each country committed to saving
one thing from extinction – them.

People wondered why it took so long.

2007 Logos

When I complain to the old man
about rising gas prices,
he says "I want $10 a gallon."

"Why?" is the obvious question.
"Because I love birds," he says.

At the time, I thought him insane
but now I think most everyone else is.

After Dreaming Extinction of Birds

Though it is hard to believe,
winged creatures
of every color and shade
filled skies with song.

One called eagle
was symbol of our nation.

One called golden pheasant
was like a painting.

One called homing pigeon
carried messages.

One called macaw parrot
spoke like a human.

Their migrations signaled
change of seasons
when there were seasons.

Desert Time Machine

Dirt roads, wrong turns, redside trout
pull me back
from the 21st century.

In general
I have no sense of time at all
so I'm always out of time

which, of course, is a blessing
or a curse
depending on who's watching

but eagles, deer, osprey
don't care
about human ways

as I have much too long.

The Self at North Fork Lake Splits into Three Selves

The first wants it all: tall blond woman, money, stone mansion.

The second, depressed, knows the Law of Impermanence means none of the above can satisfy.

The third tells the first two to shut up and notice the raven atop the ancient Sitka Spruce.

The Day I Stopped the Rape at Church Camp

The shapely freshman was drunk
and bully was ready,
taking her by the hand like a gift
into night forest.

I was behind them
on the trail
reflecting on my definition
of "love as process."

I followed them
as he tore off her sweater
then I stopped them cold.
"It's okay," she smiled.

"It's not okay
because she's drunk," I said.
The bully pushed me
and cursed,

said I could have her next,
the way oil companies today
are screwing the public.

Shad Fishers

Hundreds of anglers
and everyone catching
with no limit

makes generosity easy
as men share lures,
methods,

stories of wild days
before Bonneville
blocked salmon,

not a word
of what's coming
if poles melt,

forests into deserts
and value of human life
going negative.

In those days,
a screaming woman
will be a peacock

and climate refugees
that keep us awake,
millions of shad

from ocean waves.

Ludicrous

The bad guys of Portland Wrestling
taught us to never admit fault,

especially if we were guilty.
Kids scripted matches,

screaming at elders "What makes you think
I broke your window?"

The same way oil company execs
sold uncertainty about global warming

then years later said, yes, it's certain, but
not caused by man, and now in 2017

a few, secretly to themselves, nothing.

History Lesson

From the window in my building
people look like pixels.

Someone left a sick orchid
and two notes:

one encouraging to try,
another saying "It's not your fault."

1970s oil company bosses
understood climate change

and made war on those
trying to prevent it.

In honor of those who fight
for the community of species,

I invite you to dream each week
Lascaux and Altamira.

Climate Poem

96 million plastic "shade" balls
made from condensed natural gas
cover the Sylmar, Los Angeles, Reservoir
to stop evaporation.
News says the project helps veterans
and disabled.

It doesn't say
materials are made by oil companies
to protect us from oil companies.

Disabled Dancer

at Break Free LA,
confident,
rhythmic,
teaching us

to have no shame
moving
what must be moved,

saying
what must be said,

changing shallow
perceptions
that must be changed

to save what remains
that must be saved.

Reframe, Redefine

I remember when I learned
Safeway isn't safe
and there are no Arapahos
on Arapaho Road.

Wild trout don't call
themselves wild trout

and grizzly bears don't call
themselves grizzly bears.

How many years
did the naming monkey
fool me?

As Earth warms,
soothing words attempt
to pacify

but the ancient voice,
old as missing rain,
says look, look, look.

Water Cave Near Mogollon Rim

The baby in the womb knows the language of touch,
heartbeat, silence, movement, desire,
connection, water sphere, mother, life.

I rest in the crevasse of a watery Arizona cave,
hand on my chest and breath,
meditating on the words placenta and phoenix,

the bird that rises from ashes to live again
because soon I will be born
back into the world of those who have forgotten

where they came from, where they are now
and, like all animals, where flesh is soon going.

Indian Boy

visited my house in Tigard, Oregon, and said
"There was a lake here with fish. Where is it?"

I said when my parents bought the house, the lake was gone.
"My grandfather said it was a good place to fish," he said.

I told him Canadian geese still visited, the creek was lined
with newts and wild strawberries,

and fish ghosts from the dried lake
darted up, in, and out of my dreams.

Things I Learned at Blue River Writers Gathering

Newts move a limb at a time,
swimming through moss.

Firelight makes mundane things
like old boards beautiful.

Many scientists fear emotion, but
a split Western red cedar survives.

Ridges have spirit quest places
above steep canyons

as do ridges between people in this room.

Ancient Dwellings Near Paisley, Oregon

How would stars look if you never saw TV?
If meaning were people you dug roots with,
picked berries, hunted, fished, danced, laughed
kaleidoscope lenses of now
like an inland Galapagos hidden
except in visions and dreams?

Would you care enough
to venture beyond Facebook,
to fight with your time and words
for your children?

Near Paisley, Oregon

the ancient lake's giant
redband trout
fin small creeks.

Among swirling
ice sculptures
in thawing Chewaucan River,

I daydreamed their lateral lines
as one long red sunset
after a bad storm,

Buddhist monks
pushing children
on swings.

Ghost of Mark Twain Speaks of Climate Change

A month before
it happened,
I dreamed
my brother died

and I recalled
when we raced
across the trestle
and survived,
frosty breath billowing

like dragon hearts
and I knew,
just knew,
before long
it would be spring.

Great Horned Owl

I tried to have a conversation
with her about climate change

and she listened politely
then flew away

making me think
I should have listened more,

and watched, spoke less.
All around us, salmon,

cedar, Douglas fir,
mountain glaciers speak.

Ghost of Orwell Speaks of Climate Change

"I'm sorry I shot the elephant
but it taught me to be merciful,
unafraid
of jeering mobs, political pressure,
myself."

Seven Things I Saw Near Borrego Desert

Turkey vulture reminded me of Congress.

Waterless river – poverty.

Discarded pack of Winstons – lies.

Kumeyaay pictograph suns, humans,
and weaving – hope.

One-legged man fighting
steep trail with a walker – myself.

Cougar attack sign – failed love.

Swainson's hawk carrying snake
reminded how spirit wins
over flesh every time
and eventually flies you home.

The River That Flows Through Town

is not imaginary
though only young explorers
know it.

In tree line
along housing tract
between concrete tubes --

stick boat races,
crawfish to be caught,
raccoon tracks.

To be there
you have to turn off the TV
and go outside.

You can keep your malls,
your schools,
your after-school programs.

These hidden sections
are the only real hope
these kids have.

Message from Far Away

When people lost trees
they lost the ability to think

and minds were filled
by moneyed locusts.

Some never returned to nature
until cremated ashes

floated downriver
or were lifted by wind.

Enkidu Moment

I was casting for fall chinook in October
when the deer tore downriver, almost catching my line.
He dogpaddled for all he was worth, and his eyes begged
"Please don't tell."

I was a river hunter, not a deer hunter,
and the mixed metaphor of a salmon-deer was odd.
Orange vests emerged, excited, cursing,
crashing through alders. "Which way?" they demanded.

I thought a moment, looked at tall evergreens,
and pointed over the wrong ridge.

**Ghost of Rilke Speaks
of Climate Change**

"The river is a mirror
that changes as you change.

"An eagle flies by
then her partner

"then your shadow
unchilled, unforced."

Why I Wait

I tell my family
I'm waiting to buy an iPhone
until there are apps
that clean my salmon,
start my fire,
warm my feet
and soul,

make red Indian paintbrush,
purple lupine,
voices of unpeopled canyons,
of elders and ancients
that test you
as they were tested
and those before.

Ghost of Socrates Speaks of Climate Change

I tell him "I thought you didn't like wilderness,
that you preferred cities."

"Ghosting frees one up in ways
you can't imagine," he laughs.

"So free me up," I ask.

"That's your job," he adds,
"but I will say this:"

"Just like with the Athenian court,
I don't care about your ego or illusions,

"about your difficulty seeing,
saying, or doing right

"about the comfort of your mind,
body, or social status.

"However, your soul I'm willing
to die for, and did."

Bud Pernell's House

A story about a mule in 1909,
with block and tackle,
that pulled the McLoughlin house
in Oregon City
up a steep bluff, morphs into

a Summer Lake two story house
dragged on logs and boards by horses
eight miles from the alkaline desert
in Model T days
when townsfolk said it couldn't happen.

Both are lessons in persistence
which is needed in the Oregon Outback,
or anywhere,
as much as rain.

Broken Ritual

One year salmon didn't return to the river
and men said maybe they got lost
even though in millennia
it had never happened
to an entire run.

Wind rapped the old wood door
saying to anyone listening
"They didn't get lost. You did."

Reckoning

Even these bloody ticks,
mosquitoes, bark beetles
have their places
in the forest

but when things get
out of balance
they are like plagues
of Pharaoh.

The truth is
we blame them, but
there have been and are
too many of us.

By the Light of Dead Stars on the Oregon Coast

In a faraway galaxy it's possible
scientists mapped our CO_2 and methane curves
and know exactly
what happens next.

On a hidden beach
of driftwood and agates
you can almost feel distant prayers.

A gray evening in 1972 below farms,
apple, pear, and cherry trees,
modern kids' grandparents played
"Kick the can" until a shout
from the small blue house
"The game is over."

Warrior Says She Comes from the Land of Scalded Souls

writhing in her head
like American flags,
asks me to figure it out.

When I tell her I can't
she says U.S. History means
when we die
we meet selves
that could have been
if we had not
taken that joyride
with guys
in the stolen car.

What Happened

Truth used to live here in the age before strip malls,
and he had a dragon tattoo when tattoos were uncool.

Someone thought they saw him on a park bench,
and another time in an alley behind a dumpster.

By the time news cameras and reporters arrived
he had run away, and was nowhere to be found.

Sometimes, the old ones say, you can hear him
at sunrise or sunset when the beach is empty.

Poem for Kwas Enna

At the water filter seminar
my Cherokee friend stands and asks
"What about birds, coyotes, families
who can't afford filters?"

The salesman frowns like someone
asked about his purple underwear.

My friend continues, "Shouldn't we
make water clean for everyone
like ant people, fish people, raven people?"

"Please sit down and be quiet
or you will be asked to leave the room,"
says the irritated voice.

"Sounds to me," says my friend,
"like you already have."

Global Warming (Gary Weber) Dream

I dreamed Gary Weber forgot
to put out the fire
and by morning PLAYA Lodge
was aflame

same as he did
at his previous residency
and one before that,
a whole world smoking

and people standing
in ashes,
dried lake beds,
ghost cities,

nothing to paint on
and no one to paint to.

Scant Light

Scientists say in a billion years
the sun will oscillate
and Earth will burn.

That means as our planet
falls through space,
don't squander the gift.

Maybe as blue planets die
before their time
Great Spirit blames artists and poets

unable to convey right ideas,
in times and places,
saying what must be said

to reconnect with lost light
or awaken scant light,
or maybe artists and poets

like geese, salmon, orcas
say exactly what is needed
but leaders don't listen.

Intruder

I tell my therapist I'm upset
because a river otter hissed at me.

"You should have hissed back,"
she smiles and laughs.

"I don't want to get into a
hissing contest with an otter

"whose people were here
long before I was

"and will be after
my people are gone.

"Researchers show otters
help fight climate change."

She leans forward and says
"You have a right to be here too.

"Listen to plants, animals, birds, fish.
Don't take more than you need."

Lizard

has no formal education,
television, taxes,

like sculpture
from another planet

except for blinking eyes
maybe thinking

in Oregon's desert heat
Crickets? Mates? Shade?

Long ago or coming
apocalypse?

When Fishing Was Slow

I thought ultimately there are no fish
or fishers, river, globe, or sky –

just mere aspects of a core.
I caught my lesser self then,

filleted and ate it.
All matter is energy, ancient laws

in true unbroken light.
Someone yelled "Fish on!"

and I was back in my waders
casting.

Chilkoot

— a gold miners' trail from Alaska to Yukon

In these woods
if you shout "I'm lost"
the echo returns
through mammoth spruce
like a friend
trying to find you.

Salmon berries glow
yellow, orange
or soft red
depending on hour
and just where
light meets them.

Miles from the historic pass
rest miners' cabins
not on any map.
Through creaky doors
and unlatched windows

sun and rain
kept out for years
have gotten in
and swept the boards clean.

The Old Ones at Coastal Creek

are just stumps of former selves.
Once 200 feet tall,
now round red-fleshed nurseries
for new green seedlings
which haven't yet seen Columbus Day Storms
rolling in from the Pacific
and spawning giants that follow,
silver bright then copper
then black until ivory bones fill
deep shady pools to fertilize new roots.

Sometimes while fishing
you notice an Old One above your cast
or on the trail over your shoulder.
When you get anywhere near one
if there is sin in your life
you know it.

Turtle Island People

crawl into steel shells like mollusks
and dream spirit horses

in lavender and red clouds
thirteen thousand years ago

dancing and song,
people-magic blooming,

happier than anyone imagined
because here, like with true friends,

no matter the distance,
a natural state

so long ago in the mountains.

Exoskeleton

"If the sweet basil touches his face, he brushes it away saying,
'Hey, what's bothering me now?'" – Rumi

The psychology of being in a car has become
the dominant metaphor of our lives
so I was grateful
when my engine broke down
and I had to walk miles
along forest trails and unpaved roads
on the same paths as my leatherfoot ancestors.

Instead of NPR
I heard crows and creeks.

Instead of nothing
I smelled licorice ferns.

There was rainy mist
followed by sun
because outside Oregon is like that.

The Last Wild Otter Near Otter Crest, Oregon, 1906

"The last known native Oregon sea otter is thought to have been killed near Newport in 1906. Its pelt later sold for $900."
— Michael Milstein in Oregon Live, March 14, 2001

The autumn moon
says it's time to mate
but no amount of splashing
or singing
will bring her home
once she has gone
to that other world.

Thousands of generations
cracking open clams
with a rock on the chest,
playing in surf,
and teaching pups
secret caverns
beneath the swell

have come down to
a rich lady in New York
wearing skin
of your lover
and you, between your cries,
listening to the sound of gulls
and crashing waves
in Pacific darkness.

Sparkle

In primeval dark
as Earth cooled,

the sun knew about
Jesus and Hitler,

rise and fall of species
and civilizations,

boots on Moon,
colonies on Mars,

how many right now
are too afraid to act.

Some day when
society falls apart,

gangs run everything,
and trucks stop delivering

food and medicine,
the true cost of our lifestyle

the last 40 years
will be clear as a roadkill map

to nowhere.

Columbia River Pipe Nightmare

Legend has it above the 1240-mile pipe
there are open waters, and salmon spawn
as they have 10,000 years.

If so, the fish would have to ascend
from Astoria to Alberta
inside a tube of rainbow graffiti, gang insignias,

and a spray-painted unicorn that mocks
"I believe in unicorns."
Hawk says someone made the trek

atop the pipe to Fairmont,
saw bighorn sheep, grizzly, eagle
and finned spawning giants

pale from darkness
but still alive like our souls
hidden in cement.

One Frog

in a pot
with heat rising,

going extinct
in Brazil,

dissected
in high school,

brain scrambled
in college,

appearing as cloud
with human face

terrifying
the four horsemen:

stakeholders,
constituencies,

funding sources,
agendas.

Walking the Mountain Trail

I imagine bear hunger,
cougar eyes watching,

fluttering of humming birds,
echo rings after salmon splash.

Springtime hope of men and women
in ancient lupine.

Some say 13 billion years ago
all of this came instantly from nowhere

but the wind and I know better.

Desert Wind

says ochre and black petroglyphs
of spirals, lightening strikes, animal shapes
rooted in spirit and land
may outlast the human species
who created them.

Wind Chimes at Lazy Hummingbird Café 3/17/17

This morning China warned Trump
not to make trouble with North Korea.

Nearby, a giant black lab who could bite
your hand off licks his paw.

Chimes play louder as sparrows position
for food and territory.

I give stink eye to a kid shooting truck exhaust
while reading his phone.

One bumper sticker says "Think Before You Eat"
and another "God is greater."

Wilderness feeding this place, these people
and lessons, is falling apart.

Moonfish

My physics professor, Chuck,
makes an intentional error
on the chalkboard
and ten minutes later
yells at the class,
"Are you all on drugs?
Are you sponges?"

He looks at me,
"Starbuck, how will you
get to the moon and beyond
if you can't
figure this out?"

I tell him,
"I know there will be
colonies on Mars, but
unless they plant it
with salmon and steelhead,
I don't want to go."

Thinking About Our Space Program

It's wonderful, isn't it, how
willful and unwillful human destructions
are only for Earth and Mars,

how GE, Dupont, Monsanto,
BP, and Exxon
can't harm the Pleiades,

how, because God is good,
suffering is limited
in an unlimited universe?

Salmon Fly Fireworks

How does one return to June salmon flies
with redside trout explosions?

Not by writing about it.
Not by fish stories
among gray men
in urban fly shops
or even through prayer
beside dying fires
on winter nights.

Night Thoughts on Brain Science

I fear one day the Earth
will look like Mars

and there will be no
superheroes to save her,

Batman buried
in paperwork,

Spider-Man caught in net
of a fish trawler,

Wonder Woman in swimsuit
issue of *Sports Illustrated*

ogled by men with reptile
brains making decisions

about land, sky, water.

Things I Learned at Camp Canyonview in 6th Grade Outdoor School

Earth is a spaceship with lizards, and everything else we need.

Even nettles and mosquitoes are here for a reason.

Singing around a campfire leads to new names.

Elton John's song "Rocket Man" is really about our future
if we don't wake the hell up.

The Radical Surgery of Now

In the dream, aliens go from spaceprobe
to spaceprobe
looking for chocolate
and discarding everything else.

They've seen jewel planets
in so many spiral galaxies
The Louvre
is an outhouse to them

except somehow for Boy George
who is a kind of Mozart
in their history
where pilots sing "Karma Chameleon"

in bubble language
in weather-camouflaged ships
living personal dramas
of cause and effect

same as they did on Earth
though most everyone here
has been forgotten.

Canyon

I wanted to fish but there were cliffs,
thorns, wasps, underwater drops
where men drowned.

Two and three-foot leaping chromers,
fresh from the sea,
year after year.

Pine in air.
Blood on rocks
was fishes' and mine.

Petroglyphs and cliff trail showed
men netted here
thousands of years.

I can say more
but to know
you must go

before melting glaciers
change experiences like these
maybe forever.

Acknowledgments

Grateful acknowledgment is made to the following publications in which these poems first appeared, or are forthcoming, sometimes in earlier versions.

Amsterdam Quarterly: "Wind Spirit"
Autumn Sky Poetry: "The Last Wild Otter Near Otter Crest, Oregon, 1906"
Cascadia Review: "Message from Far Away"
The Centrifugal Eye: "The Radical Surgery of Now"
The Current: "Chilkoot"
High Country News: "Chilkoot"
Manifest West (anthology): "Canyon"
Marybeth Holleman's Art and Nature (blog): "Water Cave Near Mogollon Rim"
Miriam's Well: Poetry, Land Art, and Beyond (blog): "Seven Things I Saw Near Borrego Desert," "Things I Learned at Camp Canyonview in 6th Grade Outdoor School"
MO: Writings from the River: "Salmon Fly Fireworks"
Mobius, The Journal of Social Change: "Initiation Poem"
The Oregonian: "The Old Ones at Coastal Creek"
Otis Nebula: "Enkidu Moment"
Perceptions: "The Self at North Fork Lake Splits into Three Selves"
The Raven Chronicles: "Warrior Says She Comes from the Land of Scalded Souls" (appeared as the title "What I Think of American History")
San Diego Reader: "2007 Logos," "Geo-Poem," "How We Stopped Corporate Psychopaths From Cooking Planet Earth," "Near Paisley, Oregon," "Punch Bowl Hike Meditation," "Thoughts at the End of Empire"
Spiral Orb: "After Dreaming Extinction of Birds"

Scott T. Starbuck's Trees, Fish, and Dreams (blog): "Ghost of Bukowski Speaks of Climate Change," "Ghost of Galileo Speaks of Climate Change," "Great Horned Owl"

Through a Distant Lens (anthology): "Remembering Chief Charlie DePoe Who Loved Trains"

Windfall: "The Last Wild Otter Near Otter Crest, Oregon, 1906"

Thanks to PLAYA near Summer Lake, Oregon, for a July 2016 climate change residency that allowed me to hike trails in mountains near the Chewaucan River where I wrote most of the poems in this book. Thanks also to Greenland ice climatologist Jason Box, artists Carolyn Law, Joan Truckenbrod, Daniel Mayer, and Shelly White, archaeologist Dennis Jenkins, writers Ellen Waterston, Charles Goodrich, Karen McPherson, Charles Hood, PLAYA's Executive Director Deb Ford, and residents of Summer Lake, Paisley, and Lakeview for their generous stories and reflections.

Thanks to Blue River Writers Gathering sponsored by Oregon State University's Spring Creek Project at the HJ Andrews Experimental Forest where I revised poems in this book, and added new ones.

"Canyon" and "Near Paisley, Oregon," appeared in *Lost Salmon* by MoonPath Press.

"The Last Wild Otter Near Otter Crest, Oregon, 1906" and "Warrior Says She Comes from the Land of Scalded Souls" appeared in the chapbook *The Warrior Poems* by Pudding House Publications.

About the Author

Scott T. Starbuck wrote most of these poems at a 2016 PLAYA Art, Science, and Community Collaboration in the Oregon Outback. He was a Friends of William Stafford Scholar at the "Speak Truth to Power" Fellowship of Reconciliation Seabeck Conference in 2014, a 2013 Artsmith Fellow on Orcas Island, and writer-in-residence at the Sitka Center for Art and Ecology. His scientifically-informed poetry focuses on the clash between ancient sustaining forces like wild salmon rivers and modern industry and industrial livelihood. His climate change activism includes calling TV/news stations on behalf of San Diego area tribes in solidarity with water protectors near Cannon Ball, North Dakota, reading to over 500 climate activists at a December 12, 2016, Rally for Climate Justice in San Diego's Balboa Park, serving on the coordinating committee of the Road Through Paris action at San Diego 350.org, volunteer editing and writing at SanDiego350.org, moderating climate change film showings/workshops at his college, attending nonviolent protests, and updating his ecoblog *Trees, Fish, and Dreams* at riverseek.blogspot.com. With Antarctic CO_2 over 400 parts per million for the first time in 4 million years, and melting glaciers bringing inevitable sea level rise predicted to affect hundreds of millions of humans, he agrees with activists and creatives insisting nonviolent actions are vital now.

Fomite

About Fomite

A fomite is a medium capable of transmitting infectious organisms from one individual to another.

"The activity of art is based on the capacity of people to be infected by the feelings of others." Tolstoy, *What Is Art?*

Writing a review on Amazon, Good Reads, Shelfari, Library Thing or other social media sites for readers will help the progress of independent publishing. To submit a review, go to the book page on any of the sites and follow the links for reviews. Books from independent presses rely on reader to reader communications.

For more information or to order any of our books, visit http://www.fomitepress.com/FOMITE/Our_Books.html

More Titles from Fomite...

Novels
Joshua Amses — *During This, Our Nadir*
Joshua Amses — *Raven or Crow*
Joshua Amses — *The Moment Before an Injury*
Jaysinh Birjepatel — *The Good Muslim of Jackson Heights*
Jaysinh Birjepatel — *Nothing Beside Remains*
David Brizer — *Victor Rand*
Paula Closson Buck — *Summer on the Cold War Planet*
Marc Estrin — *Hyde*
Marc Estrin — *Speckled Vanitie*
Zdravka Evtimova — *Sinfonia Bulgarica*
Daniel Forbes — *Derail This Train Wreck*
Greg Guma — *Dons of Time*
Richard Hawley — *The Three Lives of Jonathan Force*
Lamar Herrin — *Father Figure*
Ron Jacobs — *All the Sinners Saints*

Fomite

Ron Jacobs — *Short Order Frame Up*
Ron Jacobs — *The Co-conspirator's Tale*
Scott Archer Jones — *A Rising Tide of People Swept Away*
Maggie Kast — *A Free Unsullied Land*
Darrell Kastin — *Shadowboxing with Bukowski*
Coleen Kearon — *Feminist on Fire*
Jan Englis Leary — *Thicker Than Blood*
Diane Lefer — *Confessions of a Carnivore*
Rob Lenihan — *Born Speaking Lies*
Ilan Mochari — *Zinsky the Obscure*
Gregory Papadoyiannis — *The Baby Jazz*
Andy Potok — *My Father's Keeper*
Robert Rosenberg — *Isles of the Blind*
Fred Skolnik — *Rafi's World*
Lynn Sloan — *Principles of Navigation*
L.E. Smith — *The Consequence of Gesture*
L.E. Smith — *Travers' Inferno*
Bob Sommer — *A Great Fullness*
Tom Walker — *A Day in the Life*
Susan V. Weiss — *My God, What Have We Done?*
Peter M. Wheelwright — *As It Is On Earth*
Suzie Wizowaty — *The Return of Jason Green*

Poetry
Antonello Borra — *Alfabestiario*
Antonello Borra — *AlphaBetaBestiaro*
James Connolly — *Picking Up the Bodies*
Greg Delanty — *Loosestrife*
Mason Drukman — *Drawing on Life*
J. C. Ellefson — *Foreign Tales of Exemplum and Woe*
Anna Faktorovich — *Improvisational Arguments*
Barry Goldensohn — *Snake in the Spine, Wolf in the Heart*
Barry Goldensohn — *The Hundred Yard Dash Man*
Barry Goldensohn — *The Listener Aspires to the Condition of Music*
R. L. Green When — *You Remember Deir Yassin*
Kate Magill — *Roadworthy Creature, Roadworthy Craft*

Fomite

Tony Magistrale — *Entanglements*
Sherry Olson — *Four-Way Stop*
Janice Miller Potter — *Meanwell*
Joseph D. Reich — *Connecting the Dots to Shangrila*
Joseph D. Reich — *The Hole That Runs Through Utopia*
Joseph D. Reich — *The Housing Market*
Joseph D. Reich — *The Derivation of Cowboys and Indians*
David Schein — *My Murder and Other Local News*
Scott T. Starbuck — *Industrial Oz*
Seth Steinzor — *Among the Lost*
Seth Steinzor — *To Join the Lost*
Susan Thomas — *The Empty Notebook Interrogates Itself*
Sharon Webster — *Everyone Lives Here*
Tony Whedon — *The Tres Riches Heures*
Tony Whedon — *The Falkland Quartet*

Stories
Jay Boyer — *Flight*
Michael Cocchiarale — *Still Time*
Neil Connelly — *In the Wake of Our Vows*
Catherine Zobal Dent — *Unfinished Stories of Girls*
Zdravka Evtimova — *Carts and Other Stories*
John Michael Flynn — *Off to the Next Wherever*
Elizabeth Genovise — *Where There Are Two or More*
Andrei Guriuanu — *Body of Work*
Derek Furr — *Semitones*
Derek Furr — *Suite for Three Voices*
Zeke Jarvis — *In A Family Way*
Marjorie Maddox — *What She Was Saying*
William Marquess — *Boom-shacka-lacka*
Gary Miller — *Museum of the Americas*
Jennifer Anne Moses — *Visiting Hours*
Martin Ott — *Interrogations*
Jack Pulaski — *Love's Labours*
Charles Rafferty — *Saturday Night at Magellan's*
Kathryn Roberts — *Companion Plants*

Fomite

Ron Savage — *What We Do For Love*
L.E. Smith — *Views Cost Extra*
Susan Thomas — *Among Angelic Orders*
Tom Walker — *Signed Confessions*
Silas Dent Zobal — *The Inconvenience of the Wings*

Odd Birds
Micheal Breiner — *the way none of this happened*
David Ross Gunn — *Cautionary Chronicles*
Gail Holst-Warhaft — *The Fall of Athens*
Roger Leboitz — *A Guide to the Western Slopes and the Outlying Area*
dug Nap— *Artsy Fartsy*
Delia Bell Robinson — *A Shirtwaist Story*
Peter Schumann — *Planet Kasper, Volumes One and Two*
Peter Schumann — *Bread & Sentences*
Peter Schumann — *Faust 3*
Peter Schumann — *We*

Plays
Stephen Goldberg — *Screwed and Other Plays*
Michele Markarian — *Unborn Children of America*

www.ingramcontent.com/pod-product-compliance
Lightning Source LLC
Chambersburg PA
CBHW021445080526
44588CB00009B/694